the best of grade 3
Piano

Selected and edited by Anthony Williams

FABER *ff* MUSIC

Contents

© 2007 by Faber Music Ltd
This edition first published in 2007
3 Queen Square London WC1N 3AU
Music processed by Graham Pike
Design by Økvik Design
Printed in England by Caligraving Ltd
All rights reserved

ISBN10: 0-571-52773-6
EAN13: 978-0-571-52773-1

To buy Faber Music publications or to find out about the full range of titles available
please contact your local music retailer or Faber Music sales enquiries:

Faber Music Limited, Burnt Mill, Elizabeth Way, Harlow CM20 2HX
Tel: +44 (0)1279 82 89 82   Fax: +44 (0)1279 82 89 83
sales@fabermusic.com   fabermusic.com

Anglaise in D minor

Anon.

Marche

Carl Philipp Emanuel Bach

Little Prelude in C

BWV 939

Attrib. Johann Sebastian Bach

Round Dance

from 'For Children' Vol.1 Sz.42

Béla Bartók

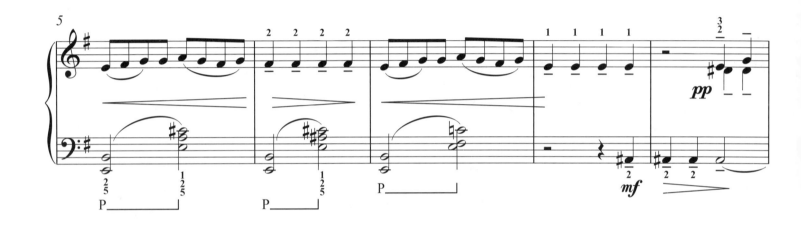

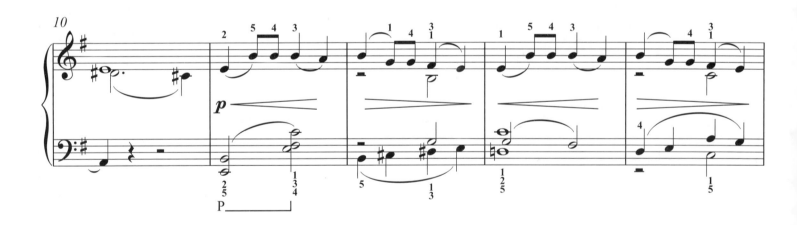

Blues in Two

from 'Easy Jazzy Piano'

Mike Cornick

Slowly, with a gentle swing ♩ = 76

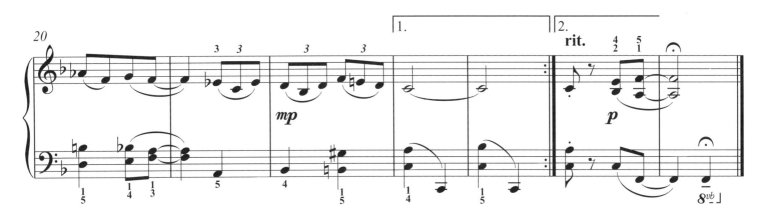

Sonatina in F

First movement Anh.5/2

Ludwig van Beethoven

Passepied

Sixth movement from Suite No.2 in D

Charles Dieupart

Gavotte in G

HWV 491

George Frideric Handel

Willow

from 'Fingerprints for Piano'

Nikki Iles

Lyrically ♩ = 108

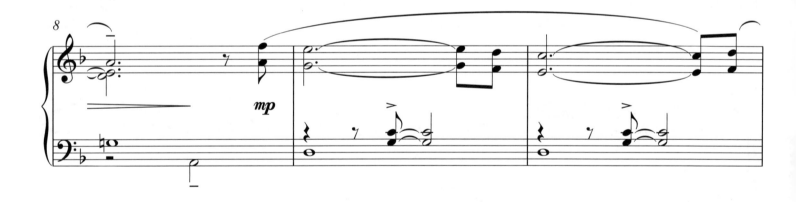

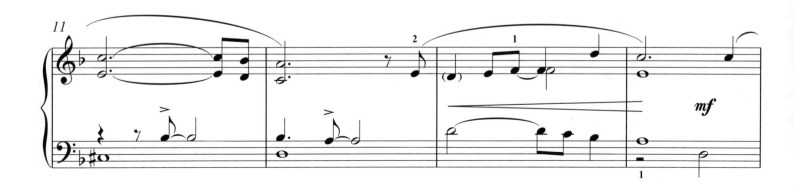

Shepherd Playing on his Pipe

Op.31 No.8

Vladimir Rebikov

Clowns

from 'Twenty-Four Easy Pieces' Op. 39 No.20

Dmitri Kabalevsky

A Passing Thought

Op.4 No.1

Samuil Maikapar

Study in A minor

Op.340 No.2

Charles Mayer

Cha-Cha

from 'Tanz-Typen' Vol.1

Siegfried Merath

Allegro in F

K.15a

Wolfgang Amadeus Mozart

Menuet in A minor

from 'First Book of Harpsichord Pieces'

Jean-Philippe Rameau

The Wild Horseman

from 'Album for the Young' Op.68

Robert Schumann

Allegro ♩. = ca 100

Old French Song

from 'Album for the Young' Op.39

Pyotr Ilyich Tchaikovsky

Molto moderato ♩ = ca 82

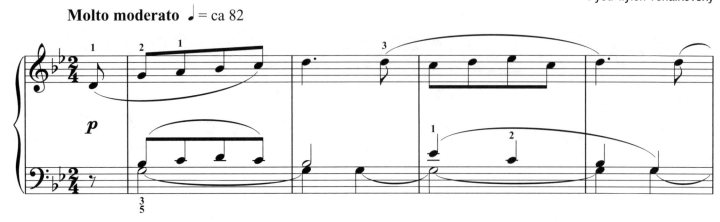

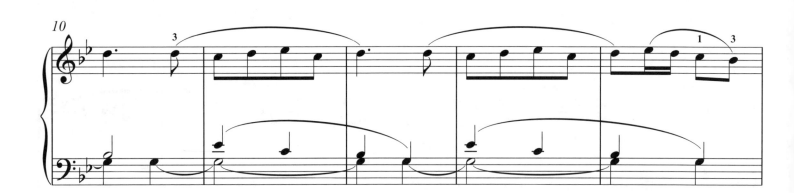

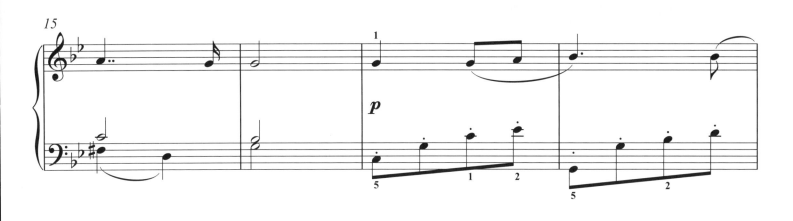

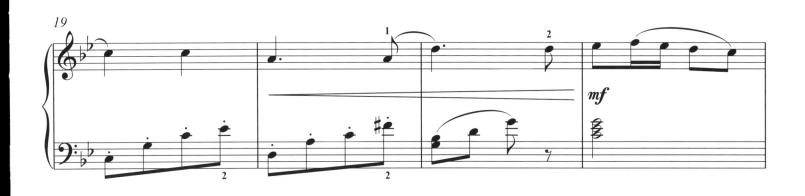

Tango III (Argentine)

from 'Easy Dances' Vol.1

Mátyás Seiber